Homeless Bird

by
Gloria Whelan

Student Packet

Written by
Sarah Nalini Mammen

Edited by
Heather M. Johnson

Contains masters for:	3 Prereading Activities
	1 Study Guide
	8 Vocabulary Activities
	5 Literary Analysis Activities
	3 Quizzes
	1 Novel Test
PLUS	Detailed Answer Key

Note

The Harper Trophy paperback edition of the book, © 2000 by Gloria Whelan, was used to prepare this guide. The page references may differ in other editions.

Please note: This novel deals with sensitive, mature issues. Parts may contain references to drug use, sexual references, and/or descriptions of violence. Please assess the appropriateness of this book for the age level and maturity of your students prior to reading and discussing it with them.

ISBN 1-58130-836-1
Copyright infringement is a violation of Federal Law.

© 2003 by Novel Units, Inc., Bulverde, Texas. All rights reserved. No part of this publication may be reproduced, translated, stored in a retrieval system, or transmitted in any way or by any means (electronic, mechanical, photocopying, recording, or otherwise) without prior written permission from Novel Units, Inc.

Photocopying of student worksheets by a classroom teacher at a non-profit school who has purchased this publication for his/her own class is permissible. Reproduction of any part of this publication for an entire school or for a school system, by for-profit institutions and tutoring centers, or for commercial sale is strictly prohibited.

Novel Units is a registered trademark of Novel Units, Inc. Printed in the United States of America.

To order, contact your local school supply store, or—
Novel Units, Inc.
P.O. Box 97
Bulverde, TX 78163-0097

Web site: www.educyberstor.com

Name _____

Homeless Bird
Activity #1 • Word Association/Freewriting
Use Before Reading

Directions: Think about each idea listed below. Then freewrite about each idea for at least five minutes. Use extra paper if you need it. Be prepared to discuss your thoughts with your classmates.

1. custom

2. critical

3. confide

4. hope

5. sacrifice

6. choices

7. unlucky

8. survival

Name _____

Homeless Bird
Activity #2 • Anticipation Guide
Use Before Reading

Anticipation Guide

Directions: Rate each of the following statements before you read the novel and discuss your ratings with a partner. After you have completed the novel, rate and discuss the statements again.

1 ——— 2 ——— 3 ——— 4 ——— 5 ——— 6
strongly agree   strongly disagree

	Before	After
1. Moving away from my parents would be fun.	_____	_____
2. I am lucky to be able to go to school every day.	_____	_____
3. It is okay to perform chores poorly when I am mad.	_____	_____
4. Girls and boys should learn the same skills.	_____	_____
5. Parents always make good decisions for their children.	_____	_____
6. I can take care of myself without help from my parents or friends.	_____	_____
7. Computers are a part of everyday life.	_____	_____
8. Patience and acceptance are always good qualities to possess.	_____	_____
9. Those who break customs can still have respect for their culture.	_____	_____
10. When a situation is cruel enough, I lose hope.	_____	_____

Name _____

Homeless Bird
Activity #3 • Geography Search
Use Before Reading

Directions: Find the following geographical locations on a map of India.

Varanasi	Ganges River	Yamuna River	Uttar Pradesh
Vrindavan	Punjab	Delhi	

Choose one of these geographical locations and research the climate, terrain, population, and other facts about the location. Based on your findings, write the script for a travel commercial and perform it for the class.

_____
_____
_____
_____
_____
_____
_____
_____
_____
_____
_____
_____
_____
_____
_____
_____
_____
_____

Homeless Bird
Study Guide

Name _____

Directions: Write a brief answer to each study question as you read the novel at home or in class. Use the questions to guide your reading and prepare for class discussion.

Chapter One, pp.1–21

1. What does Koly call her mother and father?
2. What is scarce for Koly's family?
3. How does Maa help in the struggle?
4. What is the final solution to the family's struggle?
5. What is Baap's profession?
6. How does Maa earn extra money?
7. What skill does Koly learn?
8. How does Koly handle her worries?
9. Why does Koly's older brother say Koly will not have a decent husband?
10. What does Koly want to do when they find the bridegroom for her?
11. What does Koly need for her marriage?
12. What does Maa give Koly to make the bridegroom's family happy?
13. Which of Baap's requests is not fulfilled by the bridegroom's family?
14. Why is the marriage considered a good one?
15. What does Maa think is important for a wife to know?
16. How did Koly's family choose the wedding date?
17. What is unusual about the wedding location?
18. What does Koly take with her?
19. How was Koly's family greeted?
20. What does Mr. Mehta ask for first?
21. What does Mrs. Mehta think is good about Koly?
22. What is Koly to do if she does not like Hari?
23. Where is Hari before the wedding?
24. Why can't Koly go back home with her parents?
25. What is surprising about Hari?
26. What happens to the silver earrings?
27. What would Koly rather have than a husband?

Name _____

Homeless Bird
Study Guide
page 2

Chapter Two, pp. 22–33
1. What does Koly do during her first morning?
2. What does Mrs. Mehta call Koly?
3. Why does Sass leave the house?
4. What does Koly take to Hari?
5. What is on Hari's bedroom walls?
6. What does Koly discover about Hari's illness?
7. How does Hari think he would be lucky?
8. How does Koly soothe Hari's cough?
9. What does Mrs. Mehta catch Koly doing?
10. What does Mrs. Mehta accuse Koly of stealing?
11. What does Chandra tell Koly about the marriage?
12. Who does Hari insist comes on the trip to Varanasi?
13. What does the doctor say about Hari's illness?
14. Who makes the decisions in the Mehta household?
15. Where were the healing leaves grown?

Chapter Three, pp. 34–47
1. How does the family get to the railway station?
2. How will Chandra share the sight of the Ganges?
3. What does Chandra ask Koly to do for her if Hari dies?
4. What does Koly see on the train that bothers her?
5. What makes Koly want to jump off of the train?
6. Why does Sassur give alms?
7. What structures does Koly see throughout the city?
8. Who does Koly believe Mr. and Mrs. Lal think she is?
9. What does Hari drink in hope of a miracle?
10. How is Hari transported to the river?
11. Who does Koly compare Hari to when he is playing in the water?
12. How does Koly know when Hari dies?
13. What does Sassur call Koly after Hari dies?

Name _____

Homeless Bird
Study Guide
page 3

14. Who accompanies Hari's body to the cremation site?
15. What does Sass give Koly before leaving Varanasi?

Chapter Four, pp. 48–66

1. What does the family do about Hari's room when they return home?
2. For what reasons does Sass speak to Koly?
3. Who is Koly glad to have with her?
4. Where does Sass take Koly in the village?
5. What does Sass say the papers are for?
6. What does Sass say the monthly envelopes are for?
7. Why can't Koly go home to her family?
8. What does Koly do for comfort?
9. What is the first fun thing Chandra and Koly do after Hari's death?
10. Why doesn't Chandra learn how to embroider?
11. What does Koly take from Hari's room?
12. What secret do Koly and Sassur keep from Sass?
13. Where does Koly go to be alone?
14. What does Koly imagine doing with her silver earrings?
15. What causes Chandra and Koly to dance happily?
16. How does Sass feel about Koly's work?
17. What keeps Koly from asking Sassur for help?
18. When is Sassur most happy?
19. What is Koly's favorite poem?
20. What does Koly learn from a book about Krishna?
21. What is Koly careful never to do?
22. What is the reason for Chandra's secret smile?

Chapter Five, pp. 67–78

1. What type of job does Chandra's bridegroom have?
2. What does Chandra say when Koly asks how she will love her bridegroom if she has never seen him?

Name _____

Homeless Bird
Study Guide
page 4

3. What does Chandra say when Koly asks what she will do if her bridegroom is not good to her?
4. What does Koly compare to arranged marriages?
5. How does Koly feel about Chandra's marriage?
6. What does Sass want to take from Koly for Chandra's wedding?
7. What does Koly tell Sass about the silver earrings?
8. What does Koly discover when she is in the courtyard?
9. How does Koly react to Chandra after the discovery?
10. What does Koly demand from Sass?
11. What is Koly's wedding gift to Chandra?
12. Why isn't Koly allowed to help Chandra on her wedding day?
13. What does Chandra say to Koly before leaving?
14. What, besides Chandra, disappears when she leaves?

Chapter Six, pp. 79–87

1. What does Koly hope to receive from Sass?
2. How does Koly change her work habits?
3. How does Sass react when Koly offers to comb and braid her hair?
4. What upsets Sassur?
5. What does Koly find to love?
6. Why is Sass angry about Koly's new pet?
7. What does Koly love next?
8. Why does Koly hurry away from the government office three times?
9. Why does Koly return a fourth time to the government office?
10. What does the man in his office say when Koly tells him Sass takes her pension?
11. What does the man in the office say will happen if Koly moves?
12. What would Koly need in order to leave?
13. How is life becoming more difficult in the Mehtas' house?
14. What changes Koly's world completely?

Name _____

Homeless Bird
Study Guide
page 5

Chapter Seven, pp. 88–103

1. In what ways does Chandra no longer look like a young girl?
2. Why are Sassur's thumbs tied after his death? his toes?
3. Why are pebbles dropped along the path on the way home from the funeral?
4. How does Koly know Sassur would not want to return?
5. How has Chandra been lucky as a wife?
6. How is Chandra treated by her family during her visit?
7. What does Chandra say when Koly tells her about her plan to run away?
8. What is different about Sass after the funeral?
9. How does Sass receive money?
10. What two things does Sass want to sell that matter most to Koly?
11. What does Koly let Sass sell?
12. What does the letter from Delhi say?
13. What does Sass do with the railway tickets after she buys them?
14. What "surprise" does Sass plan for Koly on the trip to Delhi?
15. What is strange about the surprise?
16. How does Koly feel leaving the Mehtas' home?
17. How does Sass feel leaving her home?
18. What does Sass give Koly at the railway station?
19. How do Sass and Koly get to the temple in Vrindavan?
20. What does Koly see everywhere on the city streets?
21. How does Sass treat the rickshaw driver?
22. What does Sass send Koly to do?
23. What does Koly think when she cannot find Sass?
24. Where does Koly decide to go when she finds herself alone?
25. What does Koly see in the eyes of the widow who gives her directions?
26. Where does the rickshaw driver say Sass went?

Chapter Eight, pp. 104–121

1. What does Koly recall that foretold Sass' plan to abandon her?
2. What advice does the rickshaw boy give Koly?
3. Why doesn't Koly lay down on the sidewalk?

Name _____

Homeless Bird
Study Guide
page 6

4. Where does Koly sleep her first night alone?
5. What reason does the elderly widow give for why families abandon widows?
6. Why does Koly decide she cannot return home to her parents?
7. What is Koly ashamed of the second night?
8. How has Sassur helped Koly?
9. Why is Koly still unable to receive her pension?
10. What does Koly fear will be Sass' final cruelty to her?
11. Why doesn't Koly chant in the temples?
12. Where does Koly go each afternoon?
13. Who does Koly see just when she begins to think she must sell her Tagore book?
14. What warning does Koly receive?
15. How does Koly escape the strange man in the street, and where does she find safety?
16. What does the rickshaw boy plan to do in his life?
17. How does the rickshaw boy see Koly's situation differently than she does?
18. Where does the rickshaw boy take Koly?
19. What is the rickshaw boy's name?
20. What does Maa Kamala say when Koly arrives?
21. What does Tanu give Koly after her rude welcome?
22. What is Tanu's goal?
23. Who gives Maa Kamala the money to support the widows' house?
24. What does Maa Kamala do when the girls are sharing their miserable tales?
25. Why does Koly feel she must hug Maa Kamala?

Chapter Nine, pp. 122–143
1. How does Koly feel her first night in the widows' home?
2. What does Mr. Govind expect from Koly?
3. What offer does the bangle booth owner make after seeing the girls' orange-stained hands?
4. How does Koly solve the problem for Mr. Govind?
5. Why is threading beads onto bangles different to Koly than embroidery?
6. How are Koly and Tanu different than the other widows in the house?

Name _____

Homeless Bird
Study Guide
page 7

7. What happens to the money the girls earn?
8. What other income does Koly have now?
9. What poems do the older widows like? What poems do the younger widows like?
10. When does Raji return to the house?
11. What does Koly do to repay Raji's kindness?
12. What are Raji's favorite poems?
13. What do Koly and Raji have in common?
14. Where do Koly and Raji go together in secret?
15. What has changed in Raji's life?
16. What do Koly and Raji see after he tells her he wants a wife?
17. Who is coming to the widow's home? Of what custom does the visitor disapprove?
18. What surprises Koly and Tanu about the visitor?
19. What does Maa Kamala ask Koly and Tanu to do?
20. What does the visitor say she regrets not being able to do?
21. What does the visitor say about Rabindranath Tagore?
22. What does the visitor believe she has found after seeing Koly's embroidered quilt?
23. What does the visitor plan for Koly?

Chapter Ten, pp. 144–164

1. What does Maa Kamala say when Koly uses the name "rich lady"?
2. What does Koly do for the first time when Mrs. Devi comes?
3. Who does Mrs. Devi say the quilt reminds her of?
4. Where does Mrs. Devi's money for the widows' home come from?
5. Why does Koly like Mr. Das immediately?
6. What does Mrs. Devi call Koly before she introduces her to Mr. Das?
7. Why is Koly grateful to her maa?
8. What does Koly tell Mr. Das after Mrs. Devi leaves the shop?
9. Why is Mr. Das dissatisfied with Koly's first embroidery design?
10. What design pleases Mr. Das?
11. How does Koly come to view Mr. Das' workroom?
12. How does Koly find a way to get her silver earrings back?

Name _____

Homeless Bird
Study Guide
page 8

13. What is Koly's only sadness?
14. Who is the Shrew?
15. When does Koly see Mr. Das angry?
16. How does Mala get away with tardiness each morning?
17. What does Mala say about Maa Kamala's house?
18. What does Mala promise to show Koly if she spends a night with her?
19. How does Koly visit Mala after Maa Kamala forbids it?
20. What does Koly borrow before going to Mala's?
21. How are the people Koly meets in Mala's room different from her?
22. What does Koly discover at Mala's?
23. How does the older artist, Kajal, trick Koly?
24. What does Tanu tell Maa Kamala to explain Koly's sickness?
25. How does Mala keep Koly from telling Mr. Das about the stolen phul-khana?

Chapter Eleven, pp. 165–182

1. Where does Raji appear?
2. What does Raji ask of Koly?
3. How has Vrindavan changed for Koly?
4. What do Koly and Raji see again at the river?
5. Why does Raji ignore his anger toward Kajal?
6. What worries Koly when she realizes Raji is proposing marriage?
7. What does Raji say he does not want to marry?
8. What two things stop Koly from accepting Raji's proposal?
9. What do Koly and Raji promise to do while they wait for marriage?
10. Where does the Shrew tell Mr. Das to look for the missing gold thread?
11. What surprise does Raji write about in June?
12. What does Koly embroider in the middle of the fourth quilt? Why?
13. What will Mr. Das give Koly if she promises to make time for embroidery in her new home?
14. Who does Koly feel sorry for during her last days in the workroom?
15. What does Koly plan for Mrs. Devi's sari?

Homeless Bird
Activity #4 • Vocabulary
Chapter 1, pp. 1–21

Name _____

fast (1)	dowry (1)	scribe (2)	muslin (4)
tamarind (5)	astrologer (8)	auspicious (8)	kilo (10)
bullocks (11)	prodded (13)	vermilion (15)	rouged (15)
petticoat (15)	fringed (17)	sulky (17)	headdress (17)
curries (18)	defied (19)		

Directions: Write each vocabulary word on a piece of paper (one word per piece). Using the circle below, make a spinner. Now play the following game with a classmate. (It is a good idea to have a dictionary and thesaurus handy.) Place the papers in a small container. The first player draws a word from the container. The player then spins the spinner and follows the direction where the pointer lands. For example, if the player draws the word "scribe" and lands on "define," the player must define the word scribe. If the player's partner accepts the answer as correct, the first player scores one point and play passes to the second player. If the player's partner challenges the answer, the first player uses a dictionary or thesaurus to prove the answer is correct. If the player can prove the answer is correct, the player earns two points. If the player cannot prove the answer is correct, the opposing player earns two points. Play continues until all the words have been used. The player with the most points wins.

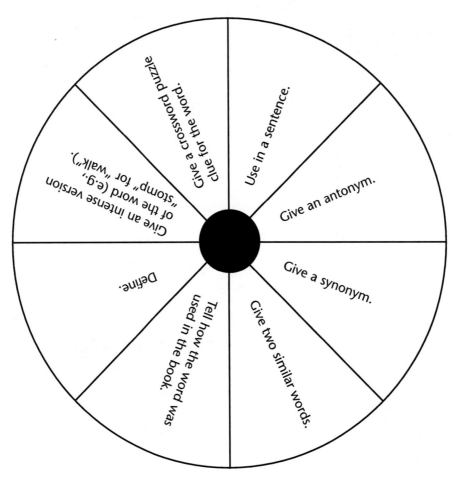

Name _____

Homeless Bird
Activity #5 • Vocabulary
Chapters 2–3, pp. 22–47

unseemly (22)	scoured (23)	sullen (27)	cunning (29)
pyres (29)	Hindus (31)	solemn (32)	tuberculosis (33)
alms (38)	rickshaws (38)	tongas (38)	shrines (38)
mosque (38)	Muslims (39)	stately (39)	camphor (40)
pilgrimage (40)	Jains (40)	Sikhs (40)	turbans (41)
saffron (41)	cremation (47)		

Directions: Select ten vocabulary words from above. Create a crossword puzzle answer key by filling in the grid below. Be sure to number the squares for each word. Blacken any spaces not used by the letters. Then, write clues to the crossword puzzle. Number the clues to match the numbers in the squares. The teacher will give each student a blank grid. Make a blank copy of your crossword puzzle for other students to answer. Exchange your clues with someone else and solve the blank puzzle s/he gives you. Check the completed puzzles with the answer keys.

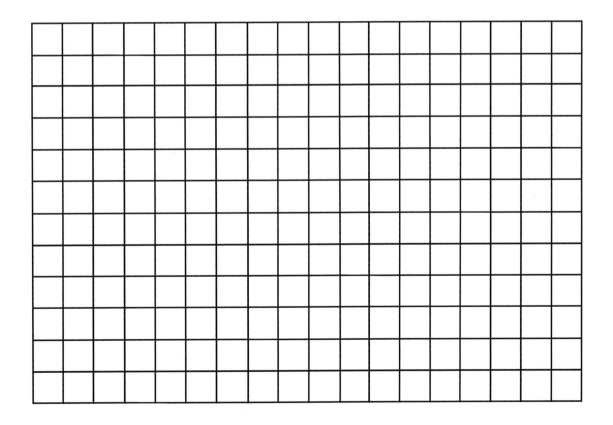

Name _____

Homeless Bird
Activity #6 • Vocabulary
Chapters 4–5, pp. 48–78

bandicoot (52)	Holi (53)	Radha (53)	modesty (56)
winnowing (58)	threshed (58)	chaff (58)	kingfisher (59)
monsoon (61)	millet (61)	gruel (62)	impudent (62)
starlings (62)	bazaar (68)	pension (71)	borne (75)
curds (76)	gawky (77)	chutney (77)	

Directions: Write each vocabulary word in the left-hand column of the chart. Complete the chart by placing a check mark in the column that best describes your familiarity with each word. Then, find and read the line where each word appears in the story. Find the meaning of each word in the dictionary. Choose ten of the words checked in the last column. On a separate sheet of paper, use each of those words in a sentence.

Vocabulary Word	I Can Define	I Have Seen/Heard	New Word For Me

Name _____

Homeless Bird
Activity #7 • Vocabulary
Chapter 6, pp. 79–87

| pariah (82) | mangy (82) | wary (82) | gosling (82) |
| veranda (83) | mynah bird (86) | shrouded (86) | |

Directions: Select five vocabulary words from above. Complete a word map for each of the five vocabulary words. Be creative when finding the magazine cut-out or drawing a symbol.

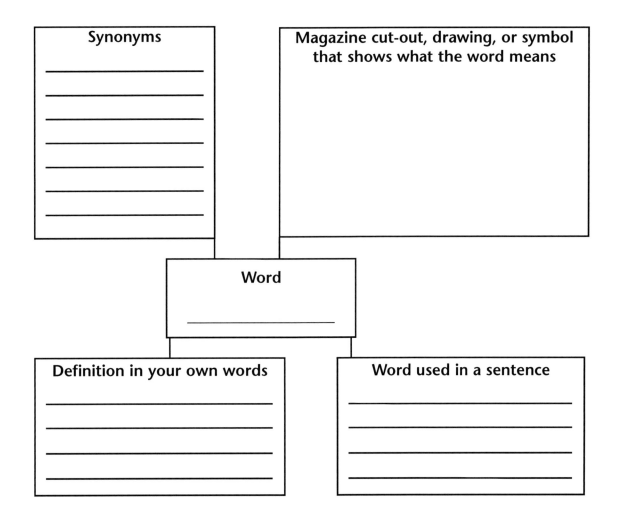

Name _____

Homeless Bird
Activity #8 • Vocabulary
Chapters 7–8, pp. 88–121

insolent (98)	vendor (100)	dusk (101)	kinship (102)
wayward (103)	monks (105)	pittance (107)	hymns (108)
pennants (111)	deity (111)	piety (111)	incense (111)
bartering (113)	inconspicuous (113)	tunic (119)	wallow (121)

Directions: Classify each vocabulary word as a noun, verb, adjective/adverb, or other. Then, select ten words and use them each in a complete sentence.

Noun	Verb	Adjective/Adverb	Other

Name _____

Homeless Bird
Activity #9 • Vocabulary
Chapter 9, pp. 122–143

bangle (126)	pacify (128)	glowered (131)	tousled (132)
dusky (137)	admonishing (138)	unadorned (139)	rarity (139)
flurries (139)	gaudy (141)	pious (141)	mournful (141)

Directions: Choose 10 vocabulary words from the list above. Write the words on the numbered lines below.

1. _____ 2. _____
3. _____ 4. _____
5. _____ 6. _____
7. _____ 8. _____
9. _____ 10. _____

On a separate sheet of paper, use each of the following sets of words in an original sentence. Your sentences should show that you know the meanings of the vocabulary words as they are used in the story.

Sentence 1: words 8 and 4
Sentence 2: words 9 and 3
Sentence 3: words 1 and 10
Sentence 4: words 3 and 6
Sentence 5: words 5 and 2
Sentence 6: words 7 and 6

Name _____

Homeless Bird
Activity #10 • Vocabulary
Chapters 10–11, pp. 144–182

ironmonger (146)	proprietor (146)	skeins (149)	deftly (154)
intricate (154)	indignant (155)	naïve (161)	modesty (165)
treacherous (166)	fertile (167)	chided (173)	corrugated (174)
smirk (176)			

Teacher Directions:

- Photocopy and cut out the following pages.
- Give one card to each student in the class.
- The student who has the card reading, "intricate—Who has the word that means innocent?" begins by reading his or her card aloud. The first card is starred.
- The student who has the card reading, "naïve—Who has the word that means fruitful?" reads his or her card aloud next.
- Play continues in this manner until all cards have been read.

☆ **intricate**

Who has the word that means innocent?

---

naïve

Who has the word that means fruitful?

---

fertile

Who has the word that means bundles of yarn?

---

skeins

Who has the word that means to grin?

---

smirk

Who has the word that means to be shaped into ridges or grooves?

---

corrugated

Who has the word that means scolded?

Name _____

Homeless Bird
Activity #10 • Vocabulary
page 2

chided --- Who has the word that means business owner?	**proprietor** --- Who has the word that means neatly?
deftly --- Who has the word that means disgruntled or irritated?	**indignant** --- Who has the word that means humility or bashfulness?
modesty --- Who has the word that means hazardous or dangerous?	**treacherous** --- Who has the word that means a person who works in the iron business?

ironmonger

Who has the word that means detailed?

Name _____

Homeless Bird
Activity #11 • Vocabulary
Cultural Word Search

Directions: Choose ten of the cultural vocabulary words in Whelan's glossary at the end of the novel. Use them to create your own word search. Switch word searches with someone else and solve them.

Name _____

Homeless Bird
Activity #12 • Metaphors and Similes
Use During Reading

Metaphors and Similes

A **metaphor** is a comparison between two unlike objects. For example, "he was a human tree." A **simile** is a comparison between two unlike objects that uses the words *like* or *as*. For example, "the color of her eyes was like the cloudless sky."

Directions: Complete the chart below by listing metaphors and similes from the novel, as well as the page numbers on which they are found. Identify metaphors with an "M" and similes with an "S." Translate the comparisons in your own words, and then list the objects being compared.

Metaphors/Similes	Ideas/Objects Being Compared
1. Translation:	
2. Translation:	
3. Translation:	

© Novel Units, Inc.   23

Name _____

Homeless Bird
Activity #13 • Character Survival
Use During Reading

Survival Chart

Directions: How does Koly survive after being abandoned in Vrindavan? What needs does one have to meet in order to survive? Complete the chart below.

Needs	How Character Gets Them
Food	
Water	
Warmth	
Shelter	
Love	
Companionship	
Mental Stimulation	

Name _____

Homeless Bird
Activity #14 • Bio-Poem
Use During/After Reading

Bio-poem

Directions: Koly is a very strong protagonist in the book *Homeless Bird*. What kind of person is she? What values does she have that you share? Using the format below, write a bio-poem about Koly.

After you have written a bio-poem about Koly, write a bio-poem about yourself using the same format. Do you think you have what it takes to make your own choices and earn your own living? Write a paragraph about the characteristics you identified in yourself.

—Line 1: First name only
—Line 2: Lover of (list three things character loves)
—Line 3: Giver of (list three things character gives)
—Line 4: Needs (list three things character needs)
—Line 5: Wants (list three things character wants)
—Line 6: Is good at (list three things character is good at)
—Line 7: Should work on (list three things character needs to improve)
—Line 8: Is similar to (list three people or other characters to whom this character is similar—list a reason behind each character, for example: Is similar to Koly from *Homeless Bird* because she is young and uncertain about her future)
—Line 9: Survivor of (list three things the character survives)
—Line 10: Last name only

Title _____

1. _____
2. _____
3. _____
4. _____
5. _____
6. _____
7. _____
8. _____
9. _____
10. _____

Name _____

Homeless Bird
Activity #15 • Foreshadowing
Use During Reading

Foreshadowing Chart

Foreshadowing is the literary technique of giving clues to coming events in a story.

Directions: Think about *Homeless Bird*. What examples of foreshadowing do you recall from the story? If necessary, skim through the chapters to find examples of foreshadowing. List at least four examples below. Explain what clues are given, then list the coming event being suggested.

Foreshadowing	Page #	Clues	Coming Event

Name _____

Homeless Bird
Activity #16 • Character Sort
Use During Reading

Sorting Characters

Directions: Similarities among characters are sometimes a clue to themes in the story. Place the following characters in one or more of the groups below: Koly, Sass, Sassur, Hari, Chandra, Raji, Maa Kamala, Mrs. Devi, Mala.

Victims	Victimizers	Fighters

Peace-lovers	Conformists	Self-directors

Name _____

Homeless Bird
Quiz #1

A. Matching

____ 1. the Mehta family's beliefs

____ 2. Koly learns this skill just like her maa

____ 3. the place where Koly was raised

____ 4. Maa works on these to earn extra money

____ 5. Sass gives Koly a white sari when Koly becomes one

____ 6. Koly looks in these hoping to learn "secrets"

____ 7. quilt, money, and silver earrings

____ 8. Hari's description of dying at Varanasi

____ 9. a fabric for clothing

____ 10. Sassur gives these to beggars for good luck

A. embroidery

B. dowry

C. schoolbooks

D. Hindu

E. alms

F. lucky

G. muslin

H. widow

I. sari borders

J. village

Name _____

Homeless Bird
Quiz #1
page 2

B. Fill in the Blank

1. Koly's baap works as a _____ in the market.

2. Maa thinks the family's welcome in the Mehtas' home is _____.

3. Sass calls Koly _____ instead of using her name.

4. The Mehtas hope the _____ leaves from the neem tree will give Hari strength for the trip to Varanasi.

5. Koly must wear a white _____ after Hari dies.

Name _____

Homeless Bird
Quiz #2

Multiple Choice: Circle the letter for the BEST answer to each question.

____ 1. Chandra tells Koly what Hari was like when he was growing up, and Koly tells Chandra about her
   (a) fights with Sass
   (b) love for Hari
   (c) own brothers
   (d) desire to go to school

____ 2. After Hari's death, Sass says
   (a) they are glad to have a new daughter
   (b) they are burdened with another mouth to feed
   (c) they will send Koly home to her parents
   (d) Koly and Chandra must be friends

____ 3. Koly begins a second quilt to comfort herself and
   (a) remember her family and home
   (b) practice her embroidery
   (c) teach Chandra how to embroider
   (d) remember Hari

____ 4. Sassur tells Koly not to tell Sass that
   (a) he apologized to Koly for letting her marry their dying son
   (b) he will help Koly learn to read and write
   (c) he let Koly take more mango blossoms
   (d) Koly took Hari's schoolbook

____ 5. Koly wants to find the courage to run away and
   (a) live with her parents in her home village
   (b) go to school to learn more from books
   (c) visit a faraway temple to Krishna
   (d) sell her silver earrings for a railway ticket

____ 6. As the family prepares for Chandra's wedding, Koly
   (a) is sad that Chandra is leaving
   (b) wishes to get married soon
   (c) refuses to help
   (d) is happy to share her silver earrings

____ 7. Sassur feels sorry for Koly when he thinks about
   (a) her old life with her parents and brothers
   (b) her being forced to wear a white widow's sari
   (c) her life without Hari and with nothing to look forward to
   (d) how the family does not have enough to eat

Name _____

Homeless Bird
Quiz #2
page 2

____ 8. Koly discovers her pension went to Chandra's dowry,
   (a) so she demands Chandra return all the money
   (b) so she begins to despise Chandra as much as Sass
   (c) but she convinces Sass to give her the pension from now on
   (d) but she makes a quilt as a wedding gift for Chandra

____ 9. Chandra's wedding is a
   (a) big celebration
   (b) small dinner
   (c) secret ceremony
   (d) family disgrace

____ 10. After Chandra leaves, Koly decides to
   (a) rebel against Sass
   (b) read all day
   (c) work very hard
   (d) go find Chandra

____ 11. Sassur says one day he will
   (a) be gone forever
   (b) quit teaching
   (c) learn about computers
   (d) tell Sass she is wrong

____ 12. The pension office says Koly needs
   (a) an address
   (b) a husband
   (c) schooling
   (d) money

____ 13. Chandra returns home
   (a) because her husband is mean
   (b) because she misses Koly
   (c) for a vacation
   (d) for her father's funeral

____ 14. Koly gives Sass her silver earrings because she
   (a) knows she does not have the courage to run away
   (b) would rather lose them than the book of Tagore's poems
   (c) knows they need food to survive
   (d) is playing another trick on Sass

____ 15. In Vrindavan, Koly feels relieved to be going to Delhi because
   (a) she will have Sass and a new family
   (b) she will not have to do all the housework
   (c) Sassur had taught her how to read and write
   (d) she will not be surrounded by thousands of other hopeless widows

Name _____

Homeless Bird
Quiz #3

A. True/False: Indicate T for True and F for False next to each statement.

___ 1. If only Koly can find the courage to go home to her parents and brothers, she knows they would welcome her happily.

___ 2. Koly returns to the railway station every day, even though she does not really believe she will see Sass again.

___ 3. Maa Kamala welcomes Koly into the home, but she will still have to search for a job on her own.

___ 4. After spending a night in Maa Kamala's home, Koly thinks she is the least fortunate person in the world.

___ 5. Koly's work stringing marigold garlands pleases Mr. Govind, so she and Tanu are allowed to make bangles.

___ 6. Raji is embarrassed that he cannot read, but he refuses to let Koly teach him.

___ 7. Raji wants to leave the city and rebuild the house on his homeland.

___ 8. The "rich lady" who gives Maa Kamala money to run the widows' home is plain and does not wear a gold-threaded sari or jewelry.

___ 9. Mrs. Devi tells Koly that her own baap's maa had been taken to Vrindavan and abandoned as well.

___ 10. The first design Koly embroiders is the heron she and Raji saw by the river, and it pleases Mr. Das.

B. Short Answer: Write a short answer to each of the following questions.

1. Why does Mr. Das' workroom become the most important place in Koly's life?

2. What does Mala say about Maa Kamala's home?

3. How is Koly tricked at Mala's?

4. Where do Raji and Koly go when he returns?

5. What two reasons does Koly have for waiting to marry Raji?

Name _____

Homeless Bird
Novel Test

A. Identification: Explain the significance of each of the following in *Homeless Bird*. Include examples of the events, characters, or symbolism related to each topic. (3 points each)

1. Sass

2. Varanasi

3. Raji

4. Maa Kamala

5. widow

6. sari

7. pension

8. literacy

9. Chandra

10. Vrindavan

Name _____

Homeless Bird
Novel Test
page 2

B. Fill in the Blank: Write the correct word in the blank. (2 points each)

1. Maa thinks the family's welcome in the Mehtas' home is _____.

2. The Mehta family believes the Ganges River in _____ will heal Hari.

3. Koly learns her _____ was the only reason the Mehtas wanted her to marry Hari.

4. The _____ finally bring Koly and Chandra relief from the oppressive heat and housework.

5. Koly becomes _____ like she read Krishna had been as a child.

6. An _____ chooses the best wedding date for Chandra and her bridegroom.

7. Koly finds the courage to talk to the government worker about her _____.

8. Sass _____ Koly in Vrindavan, the city of widows.

9. Raji and Koly go to a special place by the _____ to talk about the future.

10. Koly realizes _____ is a thief and a liar.

C. Multiple Choice: Circle the letter for the BEST answer to each question. (2 points each)

____ 1. Why is Koly willing to leave her family and marry a boy she has never seen or met?
    (a) She dreams of marriage all of the time.
    (b) She knows the family will have more food when she is gone.
    (c) She knows her bridegroom will allow her to go to school.
    (d) She does not like her parents or brothers.

Name _____

Homeless Bird
Novel Test
page 3

____ 2. Which of the following events BEST shows Koly's personality and spirit?
(a) Koly's parents tell her she is old enough to marry.
(b) Koly learns to embroider like all the women in her family.
(c) Koly asks for a photograph of her bridegroom.
(d) Koly hides under the window of her brothers' school, hoping to learn.

____ 3. Which of the following does NOT foreshadow the fate of Koly's marriage?
(a) The Mehtas do not send a photograph of the bridegroom.
(b) The bridegroom is kept hidden until the wedding.
(c) Koly's parents want to find a bridegroom for her, so they have fewer mouths to feed.
(d) The wedding is held in the bridegroom's village instead of Koly's.

____ 4. What does Hari say would be lucky?
(a) to die in Varanasi because there are many temples there
(b) to escape his village and live in a big city like Varanasi
(c) to move with Koly to their own house and raise crops in a village
(d) to die in Varanasi because his ashes could be spread over the Ganges River

____ 5. What custom is Koly forced to follow for Chandra's wedding?
(a) Koly makes a quilt for Chandra's dowry.
(b) Koly contributes money to Chandra's dowry.
(c) Koly may not see the bridegroom before the wedding.
(d) Koly may not help Chandra prepare on the wedding day.

____ 6. What does Koly believe about Sassur after his death?
(a) He would not wish to return.
(b) He would be happy to return.
(c) He would not want a big funeral.
(d) He would not want his thumbs or toes tied.

____ 7. During all of her time at the Mehtas' home, what has Koly hidden as her only hope?
(a) a schoolbook
(b) the book of Tagore's poems
(c) a red muslin sari
(d) her silver earrings

____ 8. When Koly stops one of the widows in Vrindavan and asks for directions back to the railway station, Koly sees
(a) kinship in her eyes
(b) sadness in her eyes
(c) hope in her eyes
(d) fear in her eyes

Name _____

Homeless Bird
Novel Test
page 4

____ 9. What happens during Koly's first night at the widows' home that is a great relief for her?
  (a) Tanu does not recognize the name of Koly's village.
  (b) Maa Kamala tells the widows to stop telling their miserable tales.
  (c) Tanu gives her trousers and a tunic to replace her widow's sari.
  (d) Koly learns that a rich lady supports the house.

____ 10. What is most important to Koly about her work?
  (a) Koly wants to earn money.
  (b) Koly wants to earn money for doing what she loves.
  (c) Koly wants to work with friends.
  (d) Koly wants to earn money and receive a pension check.

D. Short Answer: Write a short answer to each of the following questions. (3 points each)

1. What is Koly's favorite Rabindranath Tagore poem?

2. What does Koly feel would be Sass' final cruelty?

3. Why is Koly surprised that Raji wants her to be his wife?

4. How does Vrindavan change for Koly?

5. How does Koly feel about Sass at the end of the book?

E. Essay: Write a well-developed essay in response to one of the following prompts.

(15 points) What are Koly's personal goals? What are the main sources of motivation in Koly's life that help her continue toward her goals? How does she find hope and maintain courage despite her confining and desperate situation? Use examples from the text to support your answer.

(15 points) Why do you think Koly decides to embroider the homeless bird on Mrs. Devi's sari? Give at least three reasons and support them with examples from the text.

Answer Key

Activities #1–#3: Responses will vary.

Study Guide

Chapter One: 1. Koly calls her mother "Maa" and her father "Baap." 2. food 3. Maa sometimes goes without food, saying it is one of her days to "fast." 4. Maa and Baap arrange for Koly to marry, which will mean there is a little more food to go around. 5. Baap is a scribe. 6. Maa embroiders the borders of saris sold in the marketplace. 7. She learns embroidery, which all of the women in her family learn. 8. Koly makes her "worries stitches" as she embroiders her dowry quilt. 9. Gopal says the family is too poor to "buy" her a decent husband. 10. Koly wants to run away. 11. money for a dowry 12. a pair of silver earrings she had worn as a bride 13. a picture of the bridegroom 14. because Hari's father, like Koly's, is a Brahman, the highest Hindu caste, and he was a school teacher 15. to know how to cook and keep a house, as well as embroider 16. The astrologer picks an "auspicious date" for the wedding. 17. Instead of taking place at the bride's home, the ceremony will take place at Hari's home. 18. She takes her quilt, a sandalwood box that held the silver earrings, and a photograph of her parents, two brothers, and herself. 19. rudely 20. the dowry 21. that she will be good for work 22. learn to like him 23. Hari has the flu and is resting until the ceremony. 24. Refusing to go through with the ceremony would dishonor her family. 25. Hari appears younger than they were told, and he is thin and pale because of illness. 26. Koly hides the silver earrings behind a loose mud brick in the wall. 27. a sister

Chapter Two: 1. Koly stirs the rice and then washes the bowls and helps Sass with the milking. 2. "girl" 3. Sass goes to the village to get medicine for Hari. 4. a handful of mango blossoms 5. Butterflies and bugs are pinned to the walls. 6. Hari tells Koly that he will die from his illness. 7. Hari thinks he would be lucky to die in Varanasi and have his ashes scattered over the holy Ganges River, so his spirit will be free. 8. Koly gives Hari honey and ginger. 9. Sass catches Koly on Hari's bed showing him her quilt. 10. the mango blossoms and honey 11. that her parents arranged the marriage to get the dowry money needed to pay the doctor and take Hari to Varanasi 12. that Koly is allowed to come on the trip 13. The doctor says he has a new, incurable form of tuberculosis. 14. Sass 15. The healing leaves were grown on a neem tree.

Chapter Three: 1. a wagon 2. through Koly's darshan 3. Chandra asks Koly to make sure he has a garland of marigolds from her. 4. urns of ashes being loaded into the baggage compartment of the train 5. The train stops near her family's village. 6. Sassur gives alms to beggars because it brings good fortune. 7. shrines, mosques, and temples 8. Hari's younger sister 9. water from the Ganges 10. Two men carry Hari on a cot down to the Ganges River. 11. her brothers 12. She hears crying coming from his room. 13. a daughter 14. Only the men accompany Hari's body to the cremation site. 15. a white widow's sari

Chapter Four: 1. The family tiptoes by the room as if he is sleeping inside. 2. Sass only speaks to Koly to give an order or to scold her. 3. Chandra 4. to the government office to complete some paperwork 5. to record Hari's death 6. official business that does not concern Koly 7. It would be a disgrace. 8. Koly begins a quilt to remember Hari. 9. They celebrate Holi in the village. 10. Chandra is content to watch Koly embroider. 11. Hari's old schoolbook 12. Sassur is teaching Koly to read. 13. to the river 14. running away and selling her silver earrings to buy a railway ticket 15. the monsoons 16. Sass constantly scolds Koly and finds something wrong in every task Koly completes. 17. He leaves early in the morning and returns to work at home. 18. when he is reading 19. Rabindranath Tagore's poem about a homeless bird 20. that he was very mischievous as a child, so she too is mischievous in her work 21. never to spill salt 22. A husband has been found for her.

Chapter Five: 1. working with computers 2. Chandra says she will learn to love her husband even though she has never seen him. 3. Chandra believes her husband will be good to her as long as she is a good wife. 4. sorting through a heap of mismatched earrings and hoping to find two that match 5. sad 6. Koly's red muslin wedding sari and her silver earrings for Chandra's wedding 7. Koly tells Sass that she has lost the silver earrings. 8. Koly overhears Sassur talking about using her widow's pension from the past two years for Chandra's dowry. 9. She lets Chandra keep the money because she does not blame her. 10. that the next envelope from the government be given to her 11. a quilt for Chandra's wedding dowry 12. Only women who are not widowed and have borne a male child are privileged to help. 13. that she will miss her the most 14. Koly's happiness

Chapter Six: 1. love 2. Koly begins to rise earlier and perform all her chores perfectly. 3. Sass tells Koly she is too clumsy to comb and braid her hair. 4. Sassur is upset that computers are installed in the school, and many of his responsibilities are being taken away because he has no knowledge of technology. 5. Koly finds a mangy, pariah dog to love. 6. Sass is angry that Koly has been giving food away to a dog. 7. a bandicoot 8. Koly is not brave enough. 9. Koly gets over her fear. 10. that her family's arrangement is not his concern 11. The man tells her to go to the government office in the new town and tell them she is there. Then, the pension will come to her. 12. Koly needs courage to leave but does not feel she has that much. 13. Food is becoming very scarce in the house. 14. Sassur dies.

Chapter Seven: 1. Chandra looks more womanly because she wears a nice sari of fine muslin, her hair is in a twist, she has gold bangles on her arms, and her toenails are painted. 2. Sassur's thumbs are tied to show that he could no longer work, and his toes are tied so that his ghost could not return. 3. The pebbles will occupy the spirit so it will not follow them home. 4. He had been miserable like her and told her he would one day walk off and be seen no more. 5. Her sass is ill and does not interfere with the running of the house. She also has a servant to help with the difficult work. The house has luxuries such as electricity, a computer, and a television. 6. as a guest 7. Chandra tells Koly she would not run away. She asks Koly where she would go and who would take care of her. 8. Sass has no energy even to scold Koly, she no longer spends time with friends, she stares at nothing all day, and she does not keep her hair or sari clean and proper. 9. Sass receives some money from her own widow's pension, but she also must sell her valuables for extra money. 10. Sassur's book of Rabindranath Tagore's poems and Koly's silver earrings 11. her silver earrings 12. The letter from Sass' brother in Delhi says he will take Sass into his home if she promises to look after his children and help with housework. 13. Sass quickly puts the railway tickets away without showing Koly. 14. Sass plans to take Koly to the temple city of Vrindavan on the way to Delhi. 15. Sass has never expressed great interest in temples or practiced pujas in their home. 16. hesitant 17. Sass never looks back. 18. a palm leaf fan 19. Sass and Koly take a rickshaw from the railway station to the temple in Vrindavan. 20. widows 21. Sass rudely orders the rickshaw driver and tries to cheat him. 22. Sass sends Koly to buy two samosas. 23. Koly thinks Sass will eventually return. 24. back to the railway station, thinking that perhaps Sass had told her to meet her there 25. pity and kinship 26. on the train to Delhi

Chapter Eight: 1. the letters from Sass' brother that she had never been allowed to see, the railway tickets, and Sass' mysterious smile 2. to go and chant in the temple so the monks would give her food 3. She does not know what is allowed or what bit of sidewalk is claimed. 4. next to an elderly widow on a doorstep 5. because they bring bad luck 6. It would only bring them unhappiness and shame to discover what has happened to her. 7. Koly is ashamed when she eats while a small, hungry child stands nearby watching. 8. He had taught her to read. Now, Koly can complete the pension form. 9. She does not have an address. 10. to make her be like Sass 11. She cannot discipline herself enough to chant for hours or withstand the smells of incense and oils burning. 12. to the railway station 13. the rickshaw boy 14. The rickshaw boy tells Koly that she should not stay at the railway station because there are bad people around who look for young girls from the country. 15. by biting the man's arm until he lets her go 16. The rickshaw boy plans to return to his village where he owns land for farming. 17. The rickshaw boy thinks Koly is lucky for being rid of Sass. 18. to Maa Kamala's house, a widows' home 19. Raji 20. Maa Kamala says there is no room in the home, but that they will manage and take in Koly. 21. Tanu gives Koly trousers and a tunic to replace her widow's sari. 22. to earn enough money to share a room with some of the other girls and live on her own 23. A rich lady from the town supports the house, and the widows pay a little for room and board from their wages. 24. Maa Kamala orders the widows to stop telling their miserable tales and wallowing like pigs in mud. 25. Maa Kamala finds Koly a job.

Chapter Nine: 1. Koly feels safe. 2. Mr. Govind expects Koly to learn fast and work well. 3. to let the girls earn a bangle each to keep in exchange for their work making bangles at home 4. When Mr. Govind is angry that a shipment of jasmine blossoms arrived instead of marigolds, Koly suggests that they mix the flowers so there will still be marigolds in each garland. 5. Embroidery comes from her head and heart. Threading tiny glass beads grows tiresome. 6. Tanu and Koly are younger, stay up late giggling, and decorate their room. 7. Half of the money they earn pays their expenses at the widows' house, and the rest is put aside for them. 8. income from her pension 9. The older widows like poems about the sadness of life, and the younger widows like poems about love. 10. when Koly is reading the poem about the homeless bird 11. Koly teaches Raji how to read. 12. Raji's favorite poems are those that describe the countryside. 13. Koly and Raji both miss the simplicity of their home villages. 14. the river 15. Raji has nearly enough money to rebuild the house and buy what he needs for his crops. 16. a heron 17. The "rich lady" who funds the house is visiting, and she does not approve of the custom of widows covering their face with their sari. 18. The visitor's face is plain, and she is unadorned by jewelry. 19. to show the "rich lady" through the widows' home 20. to help more of the widows in the rest of the city 21. The visitor says Tagore is her favorite, too. 22. The visitor feels she has found an artist capable of having original ideas and is able to translate those ideas into her work. 23. to take Koly to see a maker of fine saris

Chapter Ten: 1. Maa Kamala says Koly must not call her "rich lady" because she has a name just like everyone else. 2. rides in an automobile 3. her baap, who came from a small village like Koly's 4. from her wealthy father's will 5. He reminds her of the bandicoot. 6. a gift 7. Koly is grateful to her maa for teaching her that one side of a quilt must look as good as the other. 8. that he doesn't have to take her 9. She copied what another woman was doing. 10. Koly's design of a heron 11. as the most important place in her life 12. Koly embroiders a design of silver hoops as a way of getting her silver earrings back. 13. Raji's absence 14. The Shrew is the woman who keeps a critical eye on the women in the workroom. 15. when he discovers a phul-khana has disappeared 16. Mala tells Mr. Das his competitor stops her every day to beg her for work. 17. Mala says living at Maa Kamala's house is worse than living in a prison. 18. freedom 19. Koly tells Maa Kamala that she is going to the cinema with Tanu. 20. Tanu's lipstick and kohl 21. The people Koly meets are older men and women who play music and wear sophisticated hair and makeup. They also wear jeans and T-shirts instead of saris or salwars and kameezes. 22. Koly discovers that Mala stole the phul-khana. 23. Kajal gives her a lassi laced with bhang. 24. Tanu tells Maa Kamala that Koly ate a whole paper full of monkey nuts at the cinema. 25. Mala threatens to tell Maa Kamala that Koly came to her house and took bhang.

Chapter Eleven: 1. outside the workshop 2. Raji asks Koly to go with him back to their place on the river. 3. Vrindavan was once unwelcoming and treacherous, but now Koly has found her place in it with work and friends. She is also extremely happy when she is with Raji. 4. a heron 5. because Kajal is in the past and Raji wants to talk about the future 6. Koly worries because she thinks his family would be upset if he married a widow. 7. a handful of rupees 8. Koly does not want to lose her embroidery work or her friends at Maa Kamala's house. 9. to write to each other 10. in Mala's purse

11. Raji writes Koly about the room he built in the house for her embroidery. 12. a large tamarind tree spreading its branches in all directions; to remind her of the tamarind tree back in her old village 13. a sari for her dowry 14. Sass 15. Koly plans to embroider the homeless bird from Tagore's poem on Mrs. Devi's sari.

Activities #4–#7: Responses will vary.

Activity #8: Noun—vendor, dusk, kinship, monks, pittance, hymns, pennants, deity, piety, incense, tunic; Verb—bartering, wallow; Adj./Adv.—insolent, wayward, inconspicuous; Sentences will vary.

Activity #9: Responses will vary.

Activity #10: vocabulary game

Activities #11–#16: Responses will vary.

Quiz #1: (A) 1. D 2. A 3. J 4. I 5. H 6. C 7. B 8. F 9. G 10. E **(B)** 1. scribe 2. inauspicious 3. girl 4. healing 5. widow's sari

Quiz #2: 1. c 2. b 3. d 4. b 5. d 6. a 7. c 8. d 9. a 10. c 11. a 12. a 13. d 14. b 15. d

Quiz #3: (A) 1. F 2. T 3. F 4. F 5. T 6. F 7. T 8. T 9. T 10. F **(B)** 1. Someone is paying her for doing what she loves best. 2. She says it is worse than a prison. 3. Kajal laces her lassi with bhang. 4. their place on the river 5. She does not want to give up her friends and her work.

Novel Test: (A) Responses will vary. **(B)** 1. inauspicious 2. Varanasi 3. dowry 4. monsoons 5. mischievous 6. astrologer 7. pension 8. abandons 9. river 10. Mala **(C)** 1. b 2. d 3. c 4. d 5. d 6. a 7. d 8. a 9. d 10. b **(D)** 1. the poem about the homeless bird 2. to make Koly be like her 3. She is a widow and fears his family will consider her unlucky. 4. In the beginning, Vrindavan is a menacing and unfamiliar city. In the end, Koly has found independence, friendship, work, and love. 5. She feels pity for her. **(E)** Essays will vary.